Texture and Detail in watercolour

R M Bolton
92

Texture and Detail in watercolour

Richard Bolton

B.T. Batsford Ltd • London

Typeset by Goodfellow & Egan Ltd, Cambridge
and printed in Singapore

Published by
B.T. Batsford Ltd
4 Fitzhardinge Street
London W1H 0AH

A catalogue record for this book is available
from the British Library

ISBN 0 7134 7222 7

Contents

ONE

Introduction

Watercolour is one of the oldest ways in which man learned to express himself artistically. Many centuries before Western civilizations caught up with them, the Chinese used water-based paints and inks. They revered their artists and put them on a par with their poets; each depiction of landscape shared space with an accompanying few lines of calligraphy. Art and poetry were given equal respect and value.

Many landscape artists have a particular affinity to watercolour, since it seems to echo the colour of skies and reflect back from our lakes, rivers and streams. When I first started painting in this medium, I was very impressed by the soft blends of colour and tone that could be created. Patterns and shapes could be manoeuvred into landscapes or clouds, and with a few deft strokes of a brush could be defined into a finished painting. But gradually I became less satisfied with the limitations of leaving so much to chance; I wanted to retain the spontaneity, and yet to become more involved and able to define the special attributes of my subject matter.

The bare branches form an intricate pattern against the stormy sky, contrasting well with the colours and textures of the country path (see the demonstration on pages 104-5).

The techniques I use are not new. One of my favourite methods of applying foliage, the split-brush technique, was being used by John Glover in the eighteenth century. Scratching-out and scraping can also be traced back a long way. Masking fluid is a modern creation, but some artists used to employ a technique using wax as a resist.

In my search for inspiration, I turned to the watercolours of the nineteenth century. The wealth of talent at that time was astonishing. Painters like William Henry Hunt, Sir Lawrence Alma-Tadema and John Frederick Lewis raised technical skills to a new level. John Ruskin regarded Hunt as the best role model for watercolourists. Hunt mixed Chinese White for his highlights and would even underlay his paintings with Chinese White to obtain a patina and brilliance in his colours. I have also explored modern publications by contemporary watercolourists to learn from their technique and style.

The subject matter for my paintings varies considerably. On occasion I will be taken up by landscape. As I live in flat fenland country many of my paintings reflect the scenes I find here, with lazy rivers and tall church spires on the horizon. I frequently visit Wales for a totally different scenery of hills and rocky outcrops. Water and reflections have always been a favourite theme, and living next to a river gives me the opportunity to walk its banks in all weathers and to observe its changes. The evenings are my favourite time – on a late summer's evening, when the sun casts long shadows and radiates a warm glow, the scene is cast in rich, warm colours.

Some of my paintings are of seemingly insignificant subjects. My attention may be drawn to an interesting window or an old shed at the bottom of a garden; even a bucket and spade leaning against a wall can provide material for a painting.

I find it necessary to continually re-invent my style of painting. If I have been painting large-scale paintings, I will suddenly revert to small-sized paintings. After a few landscapes I may suddenly turn my attention to garden flowers, and from there to rotting hulks in a river estuary. The sense of discovery is vital to retain a keen eye and a fresh outlook.

Surface textures have always intrigued me – old wood with its splits and weathering, or the colours and textures of rust, or ancient walls shored up with patches and rendering. Many of the richest areas of discovery for me are in people's backyards, especially farmyards where anything old and worn tends to be forgotten and pushed into a corner.

Each painting is a new challenge, an experiment in which I am attempting to capture a particular quality or atmosphere. Sometimes my work is very controlled, at other times I apply paint with vigour and freedom. The qualities are very elusive and there is always a risk element to my work. This is a positive quality – by their very nature, watercolours are never totally under the control of the artist. The unexpected effects can often enhance a painting, but equally they can negate the artist's intentions and leave him or her dissatisfied.

If a painting fails completely or I feel that I could have done better, I prop it up against the wall in my studio where from time to time it will catch my eye. Sometimes seeing a painting afresh enables me to solve the problem and with a renewed effort I can complete it to my satisfaction.

My main concern in this book will be with textures in watercolour, and with the techniques by which the artist can capture them. However, I also want to look at a related subject: the representation of detail. To paint a mass of sprawling detail can detract from the overall intention of the artist and spoil a picture, so one has to learn how to cleverly suggest detail. For example, no-one expects to paint the minutiae of every leaf on a tree, yet it is important to be able to suggest that it is a tree in full leaf.

Shed Interior
Detail from the painting on page 43. The clutter and informal arrangement of objects in this old shed attracted me. The items on the chest of drawers have been painted in detail, but not in a rigid style.

TWO

Paper

The choice of paper is an important factor. Its absorbency, texture and quality are critical in controlling the medium. The paper has to be strong enough to withstand stretching, scratching and rubbing. It has to be absorbent, but not to the point where it acts like blotting paper, and it has to retain its whiteness, unlike cheap papers that yellow with age. For these reasons nearly all watercolour papers are made of cotton pulp, which is capable of withstanding a considerable amount of abuse while providing all the characteristics of surface texture that the artist requires.

Watercolour papers fall into three categories:
1. Hot-pressed paper. A smooth-surfaced paper, least favoured by watercolourists.
2. NOT. This is the most popular range – the paper has enough texture, or 'tooth', for the painter to make full use of such watercolourists' techniques as dragging and scrubbing.
3. Rough. As its name suggests, this paper has a heavy, uneven texture. It is well suited to techniques in which the brush sweeps over the paper, leaving speckled highlights on the surface.

Surface texture varies between makes of paper. Saunders Rough is used here and helps to create the texture of the wooden panels (see page 47 for an explanation of the techniques used).

There is a wide range of papers to choose from, each with its own characteristics. Some are quite soft and woolly, others are hard and crisp. All papers are sized to give a uniformity of handling and absorbency, but some are much more absorbent than others. It is a matter of experimentation to find a paper that suits you. Paper manufacturers advertise in art magazines and they offer samples of their ranges for you to experiment on before committing yourself to buying quantities of paper.

Paper thickness, or 'weight', is another factor to consider. It can range from 100gsm (45lb) to 400gsm (180lb). Many people prefer the thicker papers of 300gsm (140lb) because these do not need to be stretched. On the other hand, thicker paper is more expensive and for those with economy in mind thinner papers are perfectly suitable. I work on paper of 190gsm (90lb) and I always stretch my paper as I like a tight, even surface to work on.

Stretching paper

The reason we stretch paper is to prevent all the ridges and cockles that form on a sheet of paper when it gets wet. These irregularities cause the washes of paint to form into pools and troughs, and make it impossible to achieve a flat, even finish. This is most noticeable when you are painting broad areas such as the sky.

To stretch a sheet of paper, you need a good solid board and gummed tape, 3.5 centimetres (1½ inches) wide. Place the sheet of paper in water, where it will expand as it soaks up the liquid. The most convenient place is the bath. If the sheet of paper is too large, roll it gently so that it gets an even soaking; never crease it. Allow the paper to soak for at least an hour to take up as much water as possible, then drain it and transfer it to the board. Dampen the gummed tape and stick it round all four sides of the paper. Leave the board on a level surface for the paper to dry out.

Most problems experienced with stretching paper are caused by the paper pulling away from the tape while it is drying out. This can be caused by uneven drying, forgetting to drain the paper before placing it on the board or poor-quality tape. If this is a persistent problem, try running a little wood glue round the edge of the paper before applying the tape.

The stretching process may seem a little long-winded but in reality it only takes a few moments. It helps if you have several boards and can do a batch of sheets at the same time.

Transfer the wet
paper to a good
solid board.
Dampen the
gummed tape and
stick it round all
four sides of the
paper.

THREE

Brushes

A good watercolour brush needs to be very flexible, with a good point that springs back to shape after each brushstroke. It should also hold a good quantity of paint and be able to withstand a lot of use.

Sable has all these qualities. The finest is the Kolinsky sable, which comes from the Siberian marten and is taken from selected hairs from its tail. Unfortunately sable is very expensive so it is well worth considering alternatives.

Synthetic-haired brushes have been around a long time. Once they were only considered good enough for use as glue brushes, but now their standard is very high and I use them a great deal. In my style of painting rubbing and scrubbing with the brush soon wears down the tip, so I favour a brush that is not going to be too expensive and yet retains most of the qualities of the sable.

I also like Japanese bamboo brushes. They look very different from conventional brushes but I find them particularly effective for the split-brush technique – this breaks up the tip of the brush into numerous points and is effective for painting areas such as foliage.

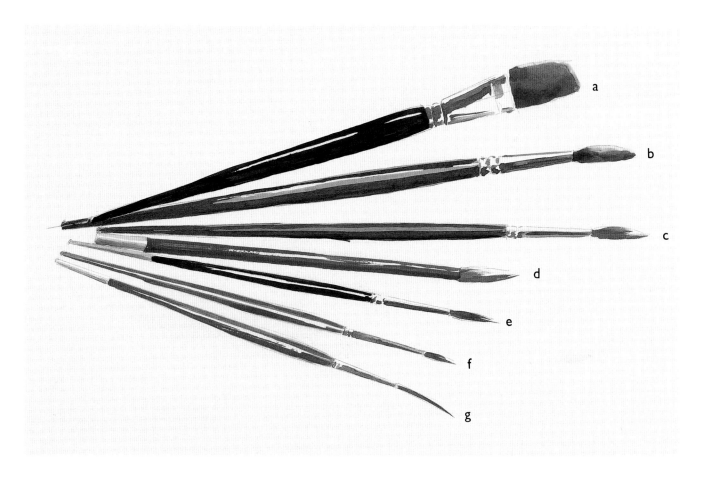

Brushes I use:
a flat ox hair brush for washes
b size 14
c size 8
d Japanese bamboo brush for scrubbing and the split brush technique
e and f both size 6 I often use these two together, one for painting, the other for softening edges with clear water; one is worn down because I use it for rough work
g rigger, for long, thin lines

One or two large brushes are required for applying washes. These can be round or flat, depending on personal preference. Sable is almost ruled out for this type of brush as the price is beyond the reach of most pockets. Again synthetic-haired brushes are a good alternative and even household paintbrushes can be put to use, especially the type used for painting woodwork.

Another useful brush to have in one's arsenal is the rigger or script liner. This is a brush with exceptionally long hairs, which was traditionally used by marine artists to paint in all the fine lines of rigging on sailing ships. It is helpful for drawing long grass and the fine branches of trees.

A small bristle brush can be used for lifting-out by scrubbing a painted area lightly with clear water and then dabbing with a paper towel or tissue to remove the paint. This technique can be used to create a highlight but is also a good way to correct mistakes.

Keep old brushes for applying masking fluid. In spite of being washed after use, the hairs eventually become clogged and useless so do not use a good brush for this.

Buying brushes

For anyone buying brushes for the first time, I would recommend buying some of the better-quality nylon brushes. I use the Winsor & Newton Cotman III series as they retain their shape well and are very resilient. A pair of size 6 brushes, which are long and round, are ideal for general painting. The reason I choose two the same size is because I use them both together, one for applying paint and the other for brushing on clear water to soften the edges of my brushwork. A smaller brush of the same series is also desirable for closer detail work. I would add to this list a size 6 bamboo brush, which can be used for many of the scumbling and rubbing techniques, and a 2.5 centimetre (1 inch) flat brush for applying washes. This brush is used for broad sweeps of wash so the type is not as critical as the finer-pointed brushes.

This selection would give an inexpensive start and can be added to as your style and experience develop.

When selecting sable brushes, take great care to choose the right shape. Most shops have a container of water available to dip them into. Check that they form a good point; you will notice that they are not identical and some may even form two points, so it is worth taking time over selection.

Care of brushes

Brushes will last longer if they are stored correctly. After use, allow them to dry out with the hairs straight. I rest mine on a raised edge to keep the tips free from all contact. Whatever you do, do not leave them at the bottom of a bag or sitting in a jar of water. When not in use, they are best stored in a brush container – the simplest is a plastic tube. Some artists prefer to keep their brushes in a folder. These are available from art suppliers but can easily be made at home. I find the simplest way of transporting brushes is in a plastic box with pull-out shelves. Many of these boxes are designed with the artist in mind and can be bought at art suppliers, but very similar all-purpose boxes from high street stores cost a great deal less and are almost as good.

A plastic box with pull-out shelves is ideal for brushes and watercolour equipment.

When not in use brushes are best stored in a brush container – the simplest is a plastic tube.

Brushstrokes

My painting technique wears brushes down very quickly despite my care of them in all other respects. I make great demands on them in creating textural effects, drawing them lightly across the paper to form a thin line or even dragging them across to leave a broad broken stroke. They are scumbled and rubbed onto the paper in different ways to produce all manner of effects. The liveliness and spontaneity of the brushwork is often the quality that brings a painting to life.

Dry brush

Most of the textural effects in my paintings are made by the dry-brush technique. The brush is kept fairly dry of paint so that paint is transferred to the surface texture of the paper rather than being absorbed into it.

The easiest way to control the amount of paint held on the brush is to remove the excess by wiping the brush against the side of the palette, and then to apply a tissue at the point where the hairs meet the ferrule; this removes excess water without removing the paint from the tip of the brush. It takes practice to control the amount of paint on the brush – there is a fine line between having just the right amount of wetness and the brush being too dry.

The technique will work with all brushes but it is very hard on the hairs and a good brush can soon become blunted, so I avoid using my newest and finest brushes for this job. My favourite brush for this technique is the Japanese bamboo brush, which is also good for stippling; as the two techniques are often combined, it makes the bamboo brush doubly useful.

Dry brush: for the most effective use of textured paper the brush should not be heavily loaded with paint.

Wet-in-wet: the brush is applied to pre-wetted paper. The paint fans out to a soft edge.

Split brush: the brush, which is kept fairly dry of paint, is repeatedly dabbed onto the paper with the hairs splayed out, to create a stippled effect.

Rigger: ideal for long, thin lines such as grass stalks and branches.

Dry brush

Wet in Wet

Split brush

Rigger

Shown opposite are some of the different effects you can achieve with the dry-brush technique:

(a) Using a size 6 brush, I first of all show the typical strokes you would expect to see from a long, round brush.

(b) The same brush is now used to build up a textured surface by rubbing it on the paper. Each time the brush needs charging with paint I take care not to overload it.

(c) The brush is moved in one direction only, letting the grain of the paper show through as a speckle of white.

(d) I have painted an imaginary cleft in a tree to demonstrate the difference between using a fully loaded brush on damp paper and the dry-brush technique, which imparts a totally different feel to the same subject.

Wet-in-wet

For soft, gentle effects the wet-in-wet technique works well. This involves brushing the paper with clear water before applying the paint. It can be used in a small patch or for the entire surface.

I use this technique constantly throughout my paintings. It is one of the greatest controlling influences available to the watercolourist because colour can be added to a painting without any brushwork – colours are simply dropped in from the tip of the brush and the paper is then manoeuvred to encourage them to drift in the desired direction. Highlights can be created by dabbing gently with a tissue and a myriad of other effects can be introduced into the wet surface. The process can easily get out of hand, colours can run in undesired directions, strange effects may need altering and ugly hard edges sometimes will form at the edge of the wet area. Rectifying the mistakes can quickly spiral into a muddy mess, which only experience and practice can help.

As a painting progresses, the wet-in-wet technique can be used in a more refined way. A tree in the distance can be painted in by dabbing the area where it is to be with water, then touching the tree in with a fine brush so that the paint spreads out to give a soft edge. It is this stage in the painting that I often work with two brushes, one charged with paint and the other with clear water. This way I can soften and blend lines as I work, exerting a considerable amount of control over the effects I am creating.

Shown here are some objects from my studio which were painted wet-in-wet, allowing colours to run together. From the

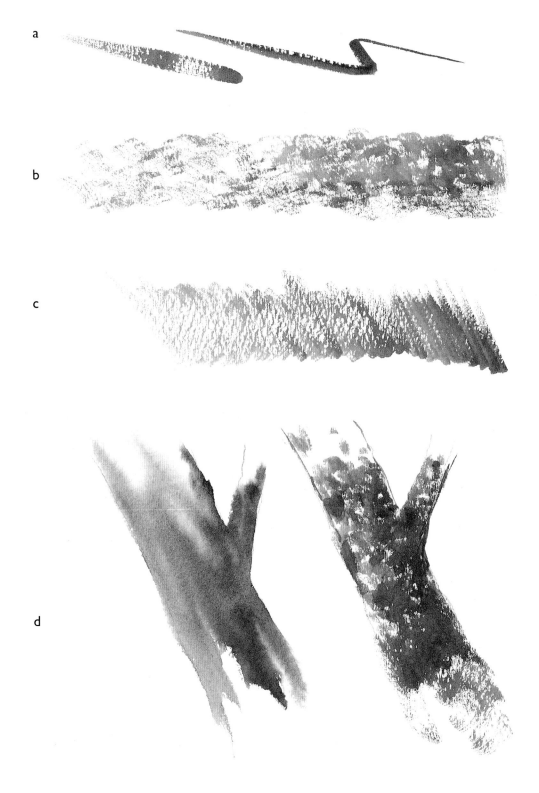

a

b

c

d

Different effects
achieved with the
dry-brush
technique. The tree
trunk is also shown
painted wet-in-wet.

The wet-in-wet technique.

jug to the paintbrushes, the same basic technique was employed – first I brushed out the subject in clear water, then added the colours.

The jug

The flank of the jug was painted with clear water, followed by a mix of Raw Sienna and French Ultramarine to diffuse into the wet surface. The spots in the glaze were made by touching the damp paper with a brushful of Burnt Sienna. The colours readily transferred from the brush to the wet paper.

The lemon

The shape was painted out in water, then deep yellow was applied to the underside and encouraged to spread upwards leaving a soft highlight at the top.

Glass bottles

Glass characteristically has hard-edged highlights so I made a point of not overpainting with water.

Highlights can be planned in advance and left as white paper, or lifted out with a brush or sponge.

FOUR

Watercolour Paints

When selecting your first box of paints, spend some time over it. There are a variety of trays to choose from — some are designed to hold tubes of paint, others are designed for pans and some can hold both. The time will come when you will want to extend your range of colours so you do not want to be restricted by the size of pans or the slots for tubes.

I have a tin box of pans, with a central aisle intended for brushes, but this space I have also filled with pans so I have a good range of colours. The reason I chose a box of pans instead of tubes was to give me flexibility; as the pans empty I can refill them from tubes. If I want a lot of colour quickly I use paint from a tube, as opposed to scrubbing at a block of colour to get enough pigment. Another advantage of my system is that I can top up the pans with paints of different manufacture instead of keeping to one make of paint.

If you are buying for the first time, select a large-sized box of paints. If there seem to be too many colours at first you can limit your range, but if you start off with a small tin it is not very easy to expand the range later. Don't feel obliged to buy

Raw Sienna

Yellow Ochre

Cadmium Orange

Cadmium Yellow
pale hue

Cerulean Blue

Burnt Umber

Ox Gall

Dioxazine Violet

Emerald Green

Viridian

Grey No. 5
Gouache

Naples Yellow
Gouache

Sap Green

Cobalt Blue

Ivory Black

Vermilion, Alizarin Crimson, Indian Red, Burnt
Sienna, French Ultramarine, Prussian Blue

artists' quality paints; the cheaper students' quality are perfectly acceptable and later, with experience, you can try expensive products.

Colours

My approach to choosing paint colours is uncomplicated. Through trial and error, I have tested colours and have finally ended up with a handful that I use again and again in my paintings. Alongside these favourite colours I have many more that I use occasionally, although sometimes I bring them to the fore as I search for new and different colour ranges. With a constantly changing palette I always have a sense of discovery, which is vital to retaining a fresh approach to painting.

Even to a beginner, it will soon become apparent that not all colours react the same way. Some colours have a high staining tendency, other colours are granular and lie more heavily on the paper – sometimes you can actually see the fine granules fall into the hollows in the paper, giving a highly textured effect. Both kinds of colour have their pluses and minuses. A graining quality would not be desirable in a sky wash but in the foreground this characteristic could be useful. Gradually, through experimentation, the possibilities of each colour become apparent and you will select a range of colours to suit your needs.

My favourite colours are Burnt Sienna, Raw Sienna, Indian Red, French Ultramarine, Naples Yellow, Burnt Umber and Viridian. As you become familiar with your paints, you will learn to select the right one for the purpose in mind. For example:

Prussian Blue A strong metallic blue with high staining capacity. It can be a hard colour to control but adds a lively quality to a painting. Mixed with other colours it can make deep, rich tones but I find it can be a bit disappointing when it dries – it loses the sparkle it had when wet.

French Ultramarine Probably the best all-purpose blue and the one I use most frequently. It mixes well with other colours and can be sponged away for highlights. Its softness makes it ideal for skies.

Cerulean Blue A light blue that has more limited use in my palette. I find it very good for mixing pale greys in sky effects.

These are the colours I find most useful.

Cadmium Orange A strong orange can be very useful. I use it mostly to give a warm glow to a painting when I am applying a wash, but it has a strong tendency to form hard edges where you least want them. The addition of a little Chinese White or Naples Yellow often helps to reduce this tendency.

Burnt Sienna A rich orange-brown. I use it again and again in my paintings to convey rust on an old tin roof, to warm up the green in dense foliage or the warm brown of freshly turned soil – a colour that cannot be readily achieved by mixing other pigments together. For winter scenes, I find myself frequently using it combined with French Ultramarine and Raw Sienna to get the greys and sombre colours typical of that time of year.

Naples Yellow This pale, flesh-coloured pigment has many uses in my palette. It can be used to give a preliminary wash, imparting an initial warm hue, and can be combined with other colours to soften them. I often use it for overpainting, mixing it with other colours to pick out details and highlights. It is particularly helpful for imparting a sense of distance where far-away features need to have their colours softened.

Viridian Most painters find the greens difficult colours to handle. Some use black and yellow to give a kind of green, while others avoid green altogether. I tend to favour Viridian, a strong, cool colour to which I add rusts or reds to attain the correct colouring for foliage. I frequently overpaint foliage with Chinese White mixed with a touch of Viridian or Leaf Green.

Overpainting

Overpainting has long been an acceptable part of watercolours. The Victorian painters developed it to a high standard, picking out highlights with Chinese White and even using it as a ground to paint on.

I use this technique in many of my watercolours in the final phase of emphasizing and strengthening features within the painting (see page 95). I have two tubes of opaque colour – Chinese White and Naples Yellow – and to these I can add any other colours in my tray to get the desired shade. Overpainting has to be applied with care and sensitivity; if it is overdone the painting will lose its transparency and will look overworked.

One other colour I have not mentioned is black. This is a colour that needs to be used very sparingly. On the whole it is

This landscape was painted primarily in translucent watercolours; gouache was used for the detail and shadows.

best to reach the right shades and hues by mixing colours, but just occasionally the introduction of black can help in producing a dark shaded area. It has a tendency to turn a painting muddy so it is often best left out of the palette.

My tray consists of twenty-two compartments and is organized so that each colour grouping is kept together. I like to experiment so I leave a couple of pans empty, enabling me to squeeze new colours into them when desired. The colours in my box are Raw Sienna, Yellow Ochre, Cadmium Orange, Cadmium Yellow, Cerulean Blue, Prussian Blue, French Ultramarine, Burnt Umber, Burnt Sienna, Indian Red, Alizarin Crimson, Cadmium Red Deep, Dioxazine Violet, Leaf Green, Viridian, Sap Green, Chinese White, Naples Yellow, Cobalt Blue and Ivory Black. One other compartment contains a block of ox gall, a useful wetting agent that can be introduced occasionally to create textural effects.

Colours are also listed in degrees of permanence, from class AA (extremely permanent) down through durable (A), moderately durable (B) to fugitive (C). This does not mean that the permanent range can be left exposed to sunlight; all watercolours will fade if exposed to light. Framed paintings should be displayed on a wall away from direct sunlight, and should be backed with an acid-free board to prevent discoloration. Unframed paintings are best stored in a paper folder.

FIVE

Techniques

I often strive to produce a particular texture or surface patina. This could be an old stone wall, a piece of weather-worn wood or a rust-encrusted piece of metal. I normally combine various effects to get the desired result, but in the following examples I have isolated these techniques to show clearly how they work. In all cases, painterly effects work best if they are planned in advance and are carried out efficiently and confidently. Overworking and muddy results are always to be avoided.

Masking fluid

Masking fluid is readily available in all art shops. It comes in a bottle and is painted onto the paper to form a barrier to subsequent painting. When it dries, it forms a rubbery layer which is easily removed by peeling or rubbing with a finger or soft eraser. It is best tested first to be sure that it will rub off your paper as some soft-sized papers can be damaged by it. Never leave it on longer than necessary as it can be very difficult to remove if left for days. I always use an old brush to apply masking fluid because the brush becomes clogged up after a time despite washing it after use.

In most of my paintings this technique is used economically to mask out a few white lines or to pick out the white spot of a highlight here and there. In fig. **a** I demonstrate the lively way it can be applied and already the possibilities of long grasses and reeds come to mind.

Masking fluid is such a useful barrier technique that it can easily be over-used. All the techniques I show are secondary to good brushwork and in my style of painting I find it important not to allow a painting to become dominated by any particular technical effect.

Scratching-out

A painting needs to be almost dry for scratching-out to be effective. If it is tried when the painting is wet, the colours will creep back into the marks and darker lines will result. Wait until the paper has stopped being shiny and wet and has become dull, though still damp, then start to scratch out. My favourite tool is a razor blade but any sharp craft knife will work; a fine line can be incised with the corner of the blade, or broad strips taken away with the edge of the blade.

With care, this technique can also be used on a painting that has dried. Apply a brushstroke of clear water and follow by scratching-out. The brush of clear water can only be applied once as further brushstrokes made on the wet paper will lift the colours.

In my example (fig. **b**) the scratching-out technique makes an interesting comparison with the masking fluid shown above. The lines are more subdued and there is a lot of character in the way paint has beaded and pooled along the lines. In contrast, the masking fluid forms hard white gashes across the paper.

Wax resist

For this technique I use a white candle stub and rub it onto the paper to impart a craggy, speckled effect (see fig. **c**). This is an imprecise technique, best suited for vague areas of texture such as the bark of a tree or an old stone wall. Used in conjunction with other techniques, it can be very helpful in creating the right patina.

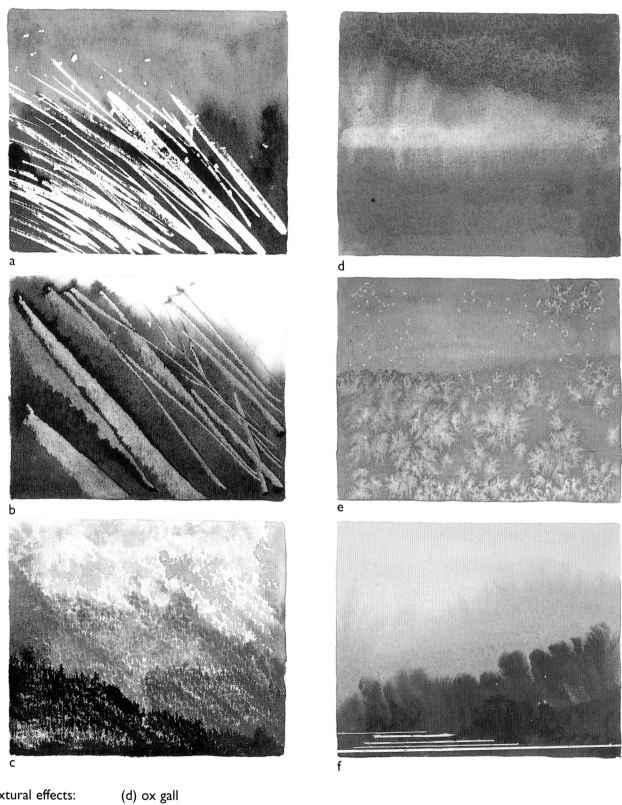

Textural effects:
(a) masking fluid
(b) scratching-out
(c) wax resist
(d) ox gall
(e) salt
(f) cutting-out or
    incising

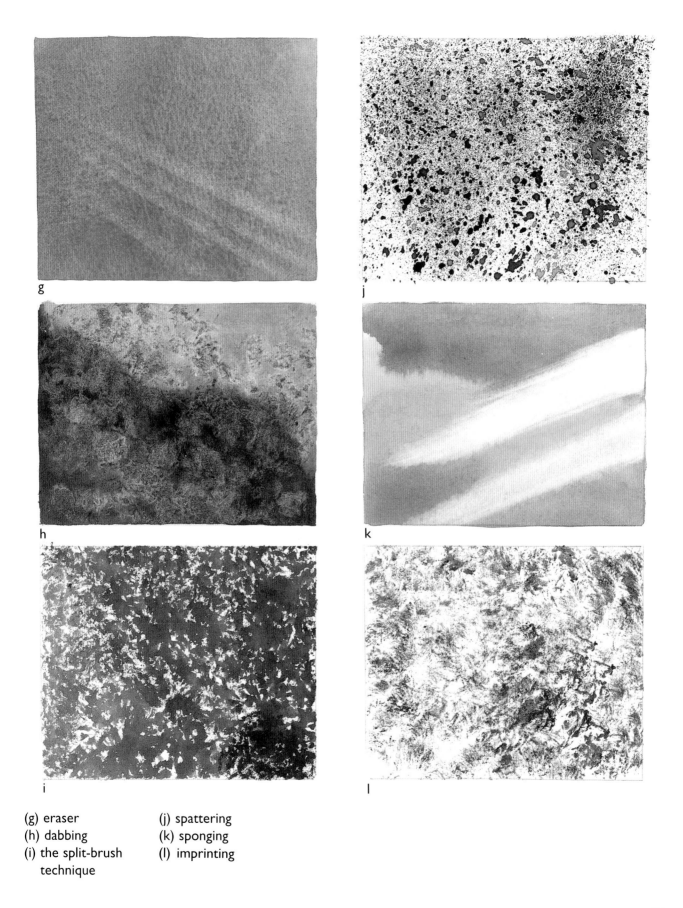

g

j

h

k

i

l

(g) eraser
(h) dabbing
(i) the split-brush
    technique

(j) spattering
(k) sponging
(l) imprinting

Ox gall

This is another imprecise technique that can be difficult to control. Ox gall is a wetting agent: applied to the surface of a wet painting, it causes the pigments to flow away from the point of application. How they flow and what strange patterns may result are hard to predict but sometimes its introduction can liven up a painting that has become dull.

If the painting is very wet the application of ox gall will cause hard edges to form, as shown in fig. **d**. For this reason, I would avoid using it for the sky because once these edges have formed there is little that can be done to remove them.

Salt

Table salt sprinkled onto the wet surface of a painting gives a pleasant snowflake effect. I have found it useful in the past for creating an impression of foliage; in fig. **e** the woolly foreground could easily be the tops of forest trees. Salt can also be used to indicate frost-covered glass and other surfaces that require a soft, speckled treatment.

Cutting-out or incising

Normally I would use masking fluid to paint out thin white lines, but another way is to cut out thin strips with a scalpel or craft knife. This requires a very sharp blade and a steady hand. I make two parallel cuts, taking care to only cut the surface of the paper, then strip the paper away from the centre of the two cuts. This technique would be unsuitable for thicker lines or random shapes. As fig. **f** shows, these lines may be just what is needed for the ripples of light on a river. The advantage of this technique is that it does not have to be planned in advance, as you have to do with masking fluid.

I have seen a similar method employed to great effect in Victorian marine paintings, where a cut was made and the edge of the paper curled over to form the curving crest of a wave.

Eraser

Areas can be lightened by using an eraser but the painting must be completely dry before this can be attempted. It is often most effective if used together with a ruler so that controlled straight lines can be erased (see fig. **g**).

For highlights on water, I sometimes use an eraser in conjunction with scraping the paper with a razor blade. Scratching the surface of the paper gently with the broad width of the razor blade, followed by the eraser, makes for a sharper speckled highlight.

Dabbing

This is most useful for developing areas of foliage. The paint is applied thickly then dabbed repeatedly with a tightly squashed-up tissue, breaking up the paint into a richly textured surface (see fig. **h**).

This technique should be used sparingly as overworking will cause the colours to become muddy and dull. Care is also needed to prevent patterns building up so the ball of tissue needs to be moved around in your fingers and twisted into different angles.

Split-brush technique

I always use bamboo brushes for this as the hairs splay out well to create the broken effect. The paint can be mixed quite thickly, as in fig. **i**, or thinly. What is important is not to have too much paint on the brush as this will form ugly blobs of colour on the paper – carefully remove excess paint back into the palette at each re-charging of the brush. This technique is quite destructive to the brush, so avoid new brushes with fine points and find an old one that will splay out to form several points.

I make a lot of use of this technique as it can be varied to form all manner of textures. The brush can be used heavily to form dark areas of foliage or almost dry, just imparting a dusting of paint to the surface of the paper. I often use it with the dabbing technique to add variety and interest.

Spattering

There are a number of ways this can be achieved. You can charge a short, stiff-bristled brush with paint and run your thumb along the bristles, making it flick droplets of paint, or just tap a normal paintbrush against a finger, causing spots of paint to hit the surface of the paper. For larger areas a spray diffuser can be used.

Some artists employ spattering to great effect, but I only use it rarely. I have one painting in this book which uses the technique extensively (see pages 124-125).

In fig. **j** I have combined spattering with a bristle brush (forming the fine stippled effect) with tapping the brush against my finger (the larger spots). Before doing this technique, mask out the surrounding area with sheets of paper as spots of paint will inevitably be sent in all directions.

Sponging

The sponge is a very useful watercolour tool; some artists use it like a brush to do much of their painting. Sponges can be used for applying washes, dabbing, stippling and lifting-out so they have universal application. Natural sponges are the best. They are soft and are capable of more delicate work than synthetic sponges. The surface texture can be used to create all manner of textures and designs.

I use sponging mostly for lifting-out, gently dabbing an area with clear water to lift an overworked section. The other technique I employ is to sweep the sponge boldly across the paper, wiping out a broad band to create a large strip of light on the surface of water or the vertical lines of a reflection (see fig. **k**). Lifting out can also be effectively achieved by scrubbing with a hog's hair brush, then applying a tissue to soak up the excess water.

Imprinting

This is very similar to dabbing except that the paint is mixed in the palette and transferred to the paper on a piece of rolled-up cloth, sponge or tissue rather than using paint already laid onto the paper.

Imprinting is useful for imparting broken textural effects (see fig. **l**) – the surface of rock, a rendered house or a light sprinkling of foliage.

SIX

Surface Textures on Buildings

The textures of stone, mortar and brick can be very effectively conveyed in watercolour. Doors and windows often make attractive compositions, especially if you focus on a detail – a potted plant in a window or a piece of decorative stonework – to bring the scene to life.

This is an ideal opportunity to experiment with techniques such as candle wax resist on Rough watercolour paper, which together help to create the patina of old stone and wood.

The textures of an old cottage are captured in watercolour and fine liner.

Battened Window

36 × 47 centimetres (14¹/₂ × 19 inches)

Windows are a favourite theme of mine. They act like a picture frame and all sorts of arrangements can be contained within them. In this case an attempt has been made to batten the window with innumerable pieces of old wood, resulting in a very unusual composition. When faced with so much detail I have to fight against my natural inclination to reach for a fine brush to define every stone and crack in the wall.

I chose a sheet of Rough watercolour paper for this painting – the textured surface adds to the patina of rough stone and wood. After drawing out the shapes, I rubbed the surface with candle wax to encourage the paint to break up. This was followed with masking fluid, painted into areas of highlight.

The first application of paint was to coat the entire surface with a wash of French Ultramarine and Cadmium Red, brushed on vigorously in all directions with no attempt at forming an even wash. While this was still wet, the darker lower lefthand corner of the painting was brushed in again, again using French Ultramarine and Cadmium Red and adding some Raw Sienna to create the dark shadowy tones of this area of the stonework.

Before the colours dried, I described the outlines of the stones in the wall. Some lines softened as they were applied to damp areas of paper, others made crisp, sharp lines. Texture and character were further developed by rubbing the brush onto the paper in the dry-brush technique. This made full use of the paper's texture as the paint was transferred to the surface irregularities, leaving the small pits in the paper as white speckles. This can be seen clearly in the lower right of the painting where the pattern of the paper is readily discernible.

To help keep the edges of the wooden battens sharp and well defined, I applied masking fluid to act as a barrier and prevent swift brushstrokes overlapping other sections. By taking this precaution the brushstrokes can be kept brisk, in keeping with the rest of the work.

Adding further to the textural effects, I loaded a brush with paint and gently tapped it against my finger, spattering spots of paint on the stonework. It is always wise to experiment on a scrap of waste paper before committing the painting to this technique. The spots can range from a fine mist to large blobs, depending on the brush and how heavily it is loaded with paint. The same technique has been employed with masking fluid to give a speckle of white dots in the darkest area.

The textured surface of Rough watercolour paper is ideal for reflecting rough stone and wood, so this was used for the painting opposite. Detail was built up over uneven washes of Cadmium Red, French Ultramarine and Raw Sienna. Textural effects were added by loading a brush and tapping it gently against a finger, spattering spots of paint onto the stonework.

Stone Wall

31 × 45 centimetres (12¹/₂ × 18 inches)

Watercolour is a very good medium for handling textures and with practice it is possible to convey many different surfaces. This is a good example of 'make do and mend' brickwork. I was attracted to the mismatch of brick and stone where a rather poor attempt had been made to brick up a pair of windows. Years of stresses on the building had caused a large crack to develop between the windows, adding to the interesting features of the wall.

I did not attempt to draw all the stones in the wall but I took care to draw the bricked-up windows faithfully. The entire surface was then rubbed with candle wax to break up the paint washes and leave some speckled highlights. Further highlights were added in masking fluid, spattering it on to add to the patina. A wash of French Ultramarine and a touch of Cadmium Red was then loosely applied to the whole surface and allowed to dry.

Detailed work started with the cracks on the wall, these being the darkest points in the painting, and from there mapping out the blocks of stone. Gradually the detail was built up, sometimes scrubbing a dry brush into the paper and at other times brushing the paint on with plenty of water to vary the textures. To make the stonework three-dimensional I added the shadows at the base of the stones, where the mortar had worn away. Finally the masking fluid was removed to reveal a variety of white lines and dots, adding to the tapestry of effects on the wall.

Watercolour and fine liner are used to create the texture and detail of an old stone wall and cottage.

Right The surface of the paper was rubbed with candle wax and highlighted with masking fluid. Detail was added and built up over a wash of French Ultramarine with a touch of Cadmium Red. A detail of this painting is shown overleaf. Note the texture on the stones and the three-dimensional effect.

Detail of 'Stone
Wall' on the
previous page.

Tintern Abbey

31 × 45 centimetres (12¹/₂ × 18 inches)

This is another example of texture and architectural detail combining to make an interesting picture. The arch and wall are very ancient but so much alteration has taken place that it is hard to visualize how the original archway might have looked. The appeal to me in painting a subject like this is the feeling of making a discovery, giving attention to something that has been discarded or overlooked. I get the same sensation from painting a piece of machinery that has withstood years of service and has built up the signs of long use.

Only a little masking fluid was required to spot in a few highlights in the stonework. I had already rubbed over the paper with candle wax to help form textural effects. Always remember to apply the wax before the masking fluid, otherwise you may have great difficulty removing the masking fluid.

The whole of the stonework was brushed over in a wash of Raw Sienna with a touch of Cadmium Red deep and allowed to dry. A further wash of French Ultramarine with a touch of Burnt Sienna was worked across the surface in a patchy style to give a suggestion of the irregular surface. Describing the detail of the wall began with the arch, built in a deep blue-red stone which can also be seen in fragments in other places on the wall. This colour was mixed from French Ultramarine and a little Cadmium Red Deep. In the wall there is a mixture of mortar, rendering and stone; the upper section is mostly rendered and this patchy quality has been made using the brush on its side and keeping it fairly dry of paint. The patches of stone vary in colours from oranges to blues and have been painted using different mixes of Burnt Sienna, Raw Sienna and French Ultramarine, with swift downward strokes of the brush. Where the candle wax has been rubbed on in a couple of places, the speckled effect it creates can clearly be seen. Further detail was done with a fine brush, for example, the rusty nails and the knots in the wood. Note how the nails have been painted wet-in-wet to achieve the soft-edged quality of rust seeping into the surrounding wood.

Detail of 'Tintern Abbey' overleaf, showing part of the arch, the wooden panels and the stonework.

Shed Interior

30 × 22 centimetres (12 × 9 inches)

I like the clutter of sheds and the informal compositions they make. Great play can be made between the dark shapes within and the view through the cobweb-covered windows.

The dark areas of this painting were treated loosely, the shapes of cans and tools suggested by blocks of tone and an occasional highlight. More detailed work was done on the objects laid out on top of the chest-of-drawers. This helps to draw the eye into the centre of the picture.

The items on the chest-of-drawers have been painted in detail but not in a rigid style; the colours have been allowed to merge softly with their surroundings. The lettering on the cans has been suggested by a few judicious strokes from a fine brush. Nevertheless the shapes are well defined and their three-

Tintern Abbey
Washes are applied over the paper which has first been rubbed with candle wax and highlighted with a little masking fluid. Details of the arch and wall are then added on top.

Shed Interior
Detail can be captured by softly merging colours together and by suggesting shapes, as in this painting where a collection of items offers an interesting composition.

dimensional qualities are sharpened by the careful placing of highlight spots on the rims of the cans, jars and bottles. The highlights were put in with masking fluid before any painting began and were rubbed away at the end to leave highlights of white paper.

The windowpanes have been left almost white; the blank open space is required to offset the jumble inside the shed. On the lower panes I have brushed in some green (a mixture of Viridian and French Ultramarine), with a suggestion of grass stems scratched in with a razor blade before the paint dried.

Spanish Window

30 × 45 centimetres (12 × 18 inches)

On holiday in Spain, I became very interested in doors and windows. Most town houses have little or no garden so people make the most of their windowsills by displaying pots of geraniums. As I looked up, each window seemed to have a different display of plant pots, laundry and cast-iron ornamentation. Caught in the sunlight, as this window was, a beautiful arrangement of light and shadow was introduced.

For me the important feature to capture was the shadow brushing diagonally across the scene, dividing it into two parts. The bright, bleached-out area in the lower half of the painting contrasted with the shadowed areas. Critical points in the painting were the geranium leaves, leaning out to catch the sun, and the bright spots of red provided by the geranium flowers – a splash of Mediterranean colour.

Much of the detail within the window area was painted out in masking fluid before I painted the geranium leaves and flowers. The cast-iron railings were also masked out as they would have been very difficult to paint round.

The whole area of the wall was painted in a very light wash of Cadmium Red, just to give a warm blush to the picture. Then the shadowed area was brushed in, mixing Raw Sienna, Burnt Sienna and French Ultramarine. The colours were applied briskly with much of the colour-mixing done on the paper. I also applied clear water, which caused the paints to

Geraniums against white plaster walls offered an interesting challenge.

run and form patterns. While the paper was still wet, I judiciously dabbed some paint away with a paper tissue to form lighter edges, then sprinkled a few grains of salt into the wet paint to create more textural effects. As the salt dissolves it leaves pale pockmarks which can be worked on later to give the impression of flaking plaster.

The framework of the window is in a darker tone. This too was painted in while the surface of the paper was still wet, causing the darker mixture of French Ultramarine, Burnt Sienna and Cadmium Red to run into the surrounding colours. Later, when dry, I gave it more definition by painting in the crack around the edges.

Turning my attention to the windows, I started at the darkest point, the gap between the shutters. This was one of the rare occasions when I used black; the small stripe was painted in a mixture of Ivory Black and Burnt Sienna. The next darkest areas were the panes of glass and they are a mixture of Prussian Blue and Burnt Sienna – the dark, icy hue of Prussian Blue is useful for mixing dark, shadowy interior views. Gradually moving forward, I painted the windows, using another blue, Cerulean (a pale sky blue), mixed with a touch of Cadmium Red and a little Raw Sienna.

The leaves of the geraniums were painted in with Viridian, adding Raw Sienna and French Ultramarine to give the right blend of colours. The leaves catching the sunlight were given a very light tint of green as I wanted to retain their sharp relief against the darker background. The final touch was to put in the splashes of Cadmium Red for the geranium flowers. The masking fluid had isolated white areas of paper, ensuring that the application of this transparent colour would retain its vibrant brilliance.

SEVEN

Metal, Rust and Weathering

Metal and rust may seem unlikely subjects for a painting, being associated with neglect and decay, but the colours and patterns you find in them lend themselves to watercolour just as much as flowers and landscapes.

Tractors and trucks have been one of my favourite subjects for many years, turning up like sculptures in remote settings. Past their useful life, they are shunted out of the way and left to rust. Discovering them amongst the undergrowth gives me the pleasure an archaeologist must feel unearthing an ancient pot.

These images call for bold colours – Cadmium Orange, Indian Red, Burnt Sienna and Sap Green. As compositions, details of abandoned vehicles and machinery open up a whole world of exciting new possibilities.

Rusty Door Handle

30 × 50 centimetres (12 × 20 inches)

I painted this close-up detail of a door panel to show how to achieve some of the effects of wood graining, rust and general wear-and-tear.

The painting was done on Saunders Rough paper, the surface of which is patterned in a myriad of little indentations. Surface texture varies greatly between makes of paper – some have very regular patterns, like basket-weave, others have more natural surfaces. I tend to prefer more natural surfaces as a patterned paper can be intrusive in a painting.

Here the Rough surface has been used to create the texture of the wooden panels. Paint is caught on the raised surface of the paper, while the hollows and indentations remain as white speckles.

The centre panel with the rusty door fitting has been treated in a different way and does not have the speckle of highlights. This section was painted with large vertical strokes followed by further 'dropping-in' of colours (see below), and was allowed to dry before being re-wetted and sponged to remove areas of colour. This helped to give the panel its dappled quality. Just before the paint dried I ran the corner of a razor blade down the paper, scratching white lines into it to mimic wood graining.

All this was done with the door fittings masked out so that my brushstrokes did not cross over into areas I wished to keep clear. When the masking fluid was rubbed away, I was left with white patches in the shape of the door handles and locks. I again used masking fluid to paint in the highlights in the metalwork, such areas as the corners of screwheads and the rim of a metal edge. Rust can be very colourful but it is difficult to get the mottled colours without them degenerating into a muddy brown. I mix the colours in the palette as little as possible and apply them to the paper with a lot of water so that they blend together naturally. Further adjustments can be made by dropping colours in or dabbing excess paint away with a tissue. To drop colours in, simply touch the wet surface of the paper with a loaded brush. The paint will run onto the paper without any need for brushstrokes, thus disturbing the existing colours as little as possible.

The colours used in this painting were Burnt Sienna, Raw Sienna, French Ultramarine, Cadmium Yellow and Cadmium Red Deep for the door handle; Cerulean Blue and Raw Sienna for the door panels; and Prussian Blue and Cadmium Red Deep for the shadows.

Opposite The texture of the wood and the rusty door handle are important elements in this painting. I used Rough paper to create the texture of the wood, and colours were 'dropped in', re-wetted and sponged, in the central panel with the rusty door fitting.

The Dashboard

62 × 42 centimetres (25 × 17 inches)

Looking at the dashboard of this old car, I was immediately struck by the rich, bright colours of the flaking paint and rust. As a composition, the arrangement of shapes and dark shadows made an unconventional but very interesting image.

The first stage was to paint masking fluid over details I wanted to keep clear – the steering wheel and bits and pieces on the dashboard. I also dabbed in some points of light down in the footwell where rust had eaten through.

I began the painting with the outside view through the windscreen. This needed to be kept simple and as light as possible to contrast with the detail and darker tones within the cab. The whole area of the windscreen was painted with clear water, then the colours were painted in to run together and blend softly. When the paint had dried sufficiently from a gloss wet to a matt damp, I was then able to paint in some lines of undergrowth which would soften out into the damp surface. If the surface is too wet, the chances are the colours will spread out too much.

To paint the cab area I started with the roof. This was painted boldly in a mix of Indian Red and French Ultramarine, with Burnt Sienna around the rim of the windscreen. While it was still wet, I sprinkled some salt into the paint to create a speckled texture.

The door pillar and dashboard were the key areas which required the most concentrated attention as the colours and textures in this section are of prime importance to the painting. The techniques I adopted were first to paint in the base colour, in this case Cerulean Blue, then to drop in other colours before the first application had dried. I did the same again with yet more colours so that one colour bled into another. As the colours began to dry I added clear water, causing the pigments to separate out and break into patterns. Eventually, when the colours had dried, I was able to work over them again, adding dark spots of rust and peeling paint.

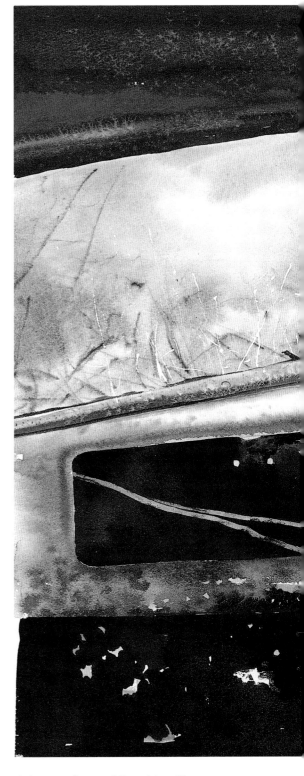

A base colour of Cerulean Blue was used to create the colours and textures of rust. More colours were dropped in before the base colour had dried.

A detail of the painting on the previous page showing part of the steering wheel and the instruments panel.

At this stage the masking fluid was removed to reveal the steering wheel and what was left of the instruments. These were now painted in, taking care not to paint over the dots and lines of the highlights. The steering wheel was initially painted in French Ultramarine and Burnt Sienna. Then, after these colours had dried, Burnt Umber and Sap Green were added by the dry-brush technique to give extra texture and colour.

The textures and details
of an old tractor are
loosely defined in this
ink drawing on wet
acetate.

Abandoned Trucks

46 × 30 centimetres (18¹/₂ × 12 inches)

With such a fragmented composition, it is easy to get carried away with detail at the expense of unity.

The main bulk of the painting was carried out quite quickly. Brushfuls of paint were applied to the paper and allowed to run together to form the foreground, while oranges and blues were run together for the large rusty shed. As much of the work as possible was treated in this way to bring a lively feel to the painting. Only when I had taken it as far as I could did I resort to finer brushes to detail the twigs and undergrowth.

Sometimes when I have finished a painting I have a sense of dissatisfaction, feeling that the painting is lacking in some respect and yet unable to place my finger on the fault. In such cases, the best thing to do is put the painting away for a couple of days and return to it with a fresh eye. That was the case with this painting. At the end of a day's work I felt that the painting was lifeless. On returning to it a couple of days later, I introduced some black, rubbing it in with the side of a brush and scrubbing in lines and tone. This final assault improved the picture.

Threshing machine,
drawn in fine liner.

Detail was applied over broad washes of colour, with a fairly rough treatment of the foreground areas.

Wheelbarrow

30 × 22 centimetres (12 × 9 inches)

This painting was made in the depths of winter, when the only green things in the garden allotments seemed to be winter cabbages. I like the blending and contrast of natural forms with hard-edged man-made creations, in this case the upturned wheelbarrow and the cabbage.

I used a wide range of techniques in this painting:

(a) The background – wet-in-wet, with a sprinkling of salt to form a speckle of white dots on the corrugated iron sheeting.

(b) The wheelbarrow wheel – wet-in-wet, followed by applying a brush to lift out paint to form the highlighted upper surface.

(c) The body of the wheelbarrow – wet-in-wet over wax resist, dabbing with a tissue to lift colours and add texture. Overpainting with gouache opaque watercolour to touch in patches of rust.

(d) The cabbage – masking fluid for the veins, then careful brushwork to describe the shapes.

(e) The undergrowth – overpainting with Chinese White and a touch of Winsor Green for the grass stems. The dead grass stems were painted in with gouache, Naples Yellow and a touch of red.

Minimal subjects can make an interesting painting, particularly if you pay attention to detail and employ a variety of techniques.

Iron Railings

22 × 30 centimetres (9 × 12 inches)

This is a curious subject for a painting as there is no particular point of interest to capture our attention. Instead there is an unusual blend of surfaces, dividing the picture up into areas of foliage, bark and rusty railings.

The regular geometric shapes of the railings are crucial to the painting. They point towards the centre of the picture, giving it some design and providing a welcome splash of colour amongst the greens and browns.

Landscapes can often be brought to life by the inclusion of some regular shapes amongst the natural forms, be it a farmhouse or a humble gate. They give a point of focus and a degree of familiarity to the scene.

Opposite Rusty railings nestling against foliage and an ivy-covered tree offer an unusual blend of surfaces.

Line and wash effectively captures the feel of old bricks in this narrow street.

58

Flywheels

29 × 24 centimetres (11 1/2 × 9 inches)

When I am drawing machinery, cars, tractors or trains I always start with the ellipses as I know these are going to be the most difficult part to get right. Once they are in place the other parts can follow. The most difficult to cope with are ellipses that are almost flat on to you, as in this picture. The curves are very subtle and require close scrutiny.

To get the gritty texture of weather-worn wood and old iron, I rubbed candle wax over most of the picture area. This breaks up the paint and adds a speckle of white dots. Next I painted out the flywheels in masking fluid. Don't make the mistake of rubbing candle wax over masking fluid as the fluid becomes very difficult to remove; always apply the wax first.

Dark areas of shadow contrast strongly with the highlighted areas of the flywheels and the old painted wood. The white lines are added to the wheel rims to make them look more solid.

When drawing an
ellipse, it often
helps to place it in
a box.

With this in place, I was able to brush in the background
of old painted wood using mixes of Sap Green, Burnt Sienna
and Cerulean Blue. The foreground was painted in a wash of
Sap Green and Burnt Sienna, which I then added to with
Viridian and French Ultramarine. When this was dry the blades
of grass were overpainted, mixing colours from my
watercolour tray with some Chinese White.

I worked in the dark areas of shadow with Prussian Blue,
Alizarin Crimson and Sap Green. Many mixes of colour will
give dark tones so it is very rarely that I need to use black.

The lighter areas were painted wet-in-wet with Sap
Green, Raw Sienna and French Ultramarine, the wax causing
the colours to break up considerably on the paper. Important
touches that make the wheels look solid are the thin white lines
round the edges of the rim. The light catches these edges and
adds a bit of sharpness.

Old Cart

35 × 24 centimetres (14 × 9¹/₂ inches)

I was very concerned that the skeletal remains of the cart would be lost if I was not careful in my treatment of the background.

To emphasize the outline of the sun-bleached timbers, I used the dark tones of a bank of trees to contrast with their whiteness. For the mottled pattern of the trees I mixed Burnt Sienna and Intense Blue and applied them to the pre-wetted paper to produce soft-edged shapes. While the colours were still wet I dabbed a tissue repeatedly into the paint, absorbing and lifting some of the paint and then transferring it to other parts of the paper.

The foreground was treated in much the same way, using Raw Sienna, Brilliant Green and Burnt Umber, only here the colours were underlaid with numerous lines drawn in masking fluid. These were rubbed away finally to produce blades of grass. I also scratched out lines with the corner of a razor blade to build up the swathes of grass.

The sun-bleached timbers of an old cart have been enhanced by placing them against a background of dark trees.

Rust and Weathered Wood
Demonstration

45 × 29 centimetres (18 × 11¹/₂ inches)

Stage 1

Before painting, I rubbed candle wax over the wooden panels and the tin roof to encourage a speckle of highlights. More precise areas of white paper were masked out in masking fluid.

The background was painted in with a wash of French Ultramarine; while this was still wet the background trees were introduced, softening at the edges as the colours mixed into the sky. The foreground was painted in Naples Yellow and Raw Sienna to give a warm base colour.

Stage 2

I could now start to build up the foreground, brushing in Raw Sienna and French Ultramarine. When the sky had dried I painted in the base colour for the roof – French Ultramarine with a touch of Alizarin Crimson.

Stage 1

Stage 2

Stage 3

Burnt Sienna, French Ultramarine and Sap Green were brushed into the foreground to describe the dense undergrowth. I flicked the brush upwards at varying angles to give the impression of grass stems.

The side of the shed was brushed in roughly with a mix of Raw Sienna and French Ultramarine. Before this was dry, I scratched in the grain lines with the corner of a razor blade. Then, while this was drying, I painted in the darkest sections, such as the shadow underneath the eaves and the doorway.

Stage 4

I now started to build up the textures on the shed wall, scrubbing in some Sap Green and Raw Sienna. The panels were given detail by painting in cracks, shadows and rusty nail holes. I tried to work with economy so that this area would not become overworked. When dry, the masking fluid was removed.

Stage 3

Stage 4

Stage 5

The final stage involved painting in the roof, mixing Burnt Sienna with touches of red and yellows. The paint was applied with a size 6 brush pressed hard against the paper and dragged down in lines so that the paint was transferred in a broken, irregular fashion. I followed the pencil lines I had drawn in earlier so that my painted lines did not go off course.

Further work was done on the side panels. More Sap Green was brushed in followed by rusts and a little more French Ultramarine. While the surface was still wet I scratched out some more grain lines.

The foreground was finished by overpainting in gouache, mixing Naples Yellow with Raw Sienna and applying the paint with a rigger brush, which is ideal for creating very thin lines like grass stems.

Stage 5 – the finished painting

EIGHT

Trees

For the landscape painter trees are essential. At a distance they can be treated as vague silhouettes, but in the middle distance or in the foreground they require more observation for a convincing rendering. There is no set procedure so techniques need to be adaptable to convey an image of foliage and the structure of branches.

The examples opposite show the variety of brushstrokes I use to give the impression of foliage:

(a) The foliage on this twisted tree has been created by using the heel of the brush. With a rich mix of colour, I first of all remove excess paint back into the palette, then apply the brush heavily onto the paper so that the paint is rubbed on via the heel of the brush rather than the tip. This technique produces a grainy, broken surface.

(b) Some types of foliage appear to be more transparent, allowing the sun to shine through the leaves. This is common in the spring before the leaves have fully developed into a dense canopy. This quality has been achieved by using a much thinner, transparent mix of colour, brushed on in a series of downward strokes.

A variety of techniques can be used to give an impression of foliage and to convey the structure of trees and branches. Here are a few examples.

Each brushstroke is strongest at its start, thinning as it reaches the centre of the tree. It is important to make swift, decisive strokes for best results.

(c) The dappled foliage of this riverside willow was created by the split-brush technique. For this I always use a Japanese bamboo brush that looks worn out but works well. I use a rich mix of colour and remove excess paint from the brush. The brush is then pressed firmly onto the paper, causing the bristles to splay out into a number of small painting tips which can then be repeatedly dabbed to build up the patina of leaves. This technique may sound a little crude but in fact a lot of control can be exerted over it and very fine, delicate foliage can be built up.

(d) Foliage often presents us with dense, heavy areas of shadow which can be blocked in with a mix of colours. It helps to give some shape to these areas by a little overpainting with a fine brush to pick out some of the leaves that are catching the light. In this example I have used a fine brush, though on a large painting I might use the split-brush technique.

A selection of trees showing their network of branches.

Branches

Painting branches sets us another challenge. Each type of tree has a pattern to its structure; what at first appears to be a haphazard growth formation actually works to a formula. An oak has one set of characteristics and a willow another. When you are painting branches, look for the habit of growth. Note how the branches separate and the manner in which they curve and twist. Once the underlying pattern is understood, it is easier to portray them convincingly. I have shown typical examples of a number of different trees above.

This drawing of a country path was carried out using a 4B pencil. The nearer branches were drawn in firmly, while lighter strokes were used to indicate trees and branches in the distance.

Tree Reflection

50 × 62 centimetres (20 × 25 inches)

We tend to think of tree trunks as either brown or grey but they can be almost any colour. The tree in the painting overleaf is catching the last rays of the sun and is bathed in yellows and oranges. Before painting, I rubbed a little candle wax around the main trunk area to encourage a speckle of white highlights.

I started painting the branches from the lower spurs outwards; the outer twigs were drawn in with the tip of the brush. Care was taken to vary the tones to give shape. With the main base colour in place, I started to work on the shadows with a mix of Cadmium Red, Burnt Sienna and French Ultramarine, continually softening the edges as I worked by running a brush of clear water along the edges of wet paint.

The foliage was painted with the split-brush technique, where I used an old Japanese bamboo brush that readily splays out at the end to impart the tiny dots of paint. The warm rays of the sun also caught many of the leaves so I used a lot of Cadmium Orange with a touch of Leaf Green to get the correct colouring.

The reflection was brushed in swiftly, scrubbing the foliage with the bamboo brush to retain a somewhat darker, flatter version of the image above. Finally a little judicious overpainting in gouache picked out the green reeds and strands of dead grass on the bank.

**Opposite
The Banks at Houghton Meadow (15 × 22cm/ 6 × 9ins)**
This small painting captures the warmth of a sunny winter's day. The soft colours of the bank of reeds in the foreground were created by adding a touch of Naples Yellow to the colours. This is a useful way of adding a soft warmth to a painting.

Detail of 'Tree Reflection' overleaf.

Detail of the painting opposite showing the split-brush technique, which is ideal for depicting foliage.

Tree Reflection The setting sun cast a glow on this tree, bathing it in warm yellows and oranges. I used a split-brush technique for the foliage and brushed the reflection in swiftly.

Archway of Trees

50 × 31 centimetres (20 × 12½ inches)

I was attracted to this scene by the overhang of trees, creating a mysterious corridor along the length of the river. I wanted to convey the feeling of dense undergrowth without resorting to painting every twig and blade of grass. This was achieved by brushing in the background colours wet-in-wet so that the soft-edged shapes could be interpreted as banks of undergrowth. The colours used were Raw Sienna, Burnt Sienna, Sap Green and French Ultramarine.

On top of these washes I began to paint in the maze of branches, using the same range of colours but adding Burnt Umber for the darker shadows. My technique for painting branches is to apply the paint to the underside of the branch, which is the area in shade, then to run a wet brush against it so that the paint creeps up and gives each branch roundness. A rigger paint brush was introduced for the fine wispy lines of the twigs. Some were painted in body colour, mixing in a little white to give a pale grey.

The shingle riverbed was first touched in with masking fluid to give a sprinkling of highlights amongst the stones, then

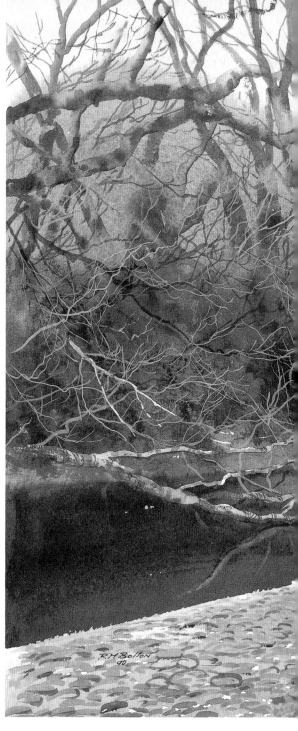

Detail of the painting above. Note how the roundness of the branches is conveyed. The underside of the branch is painted, then the top edge is softened by running a wet brush along the edge of the wet paint.

brushed over with a mixture of French Ultramarine and Burnt
Sienna. Further highlights were lifted out with a damp brush.
The dark tones of the river are a mix of Burnt Umber and
French Ultramarine, with the branch reflection lifted out by
using a wet brush.

Overgrown Gateway

20 × 27 centimetres (8 × 11 inches)

Trees can often be used to frame a scene. In the picture opposite the dark contours of the tree and the dark foreground have the effect of funneling our vision towards the view through the gate.

Much of the painting is very dark and this can lead to problems of overworking and muddy colours. I find the best way to avoid this is to mix the colours as little as possible in the palette and on the paper. I also try to return to a section already painted and re-work it as the clarity of the first brushstrokes can seldom be retained.

This painting is a good example of wax resist. You can see quite clearly the speckle of highlights just below the gate and on the bark of the trees.

This landscape with its winter trees was drawn with a technical pen.

Opposite The tree here serves to frame the painting and lead our eyes towards the view through the gate. Wax resist has been used to create highlights on the tree bark and in the foreground.

R H Bolton

NINE

Flowers

Most of my flower paintings are made in the garden as I like the informal arrangement I find there. I choose scenes where weeds and garden plants vie for attention, struggling for space in my cluttered borders. My favourite time of the year for flower painting is autumn, when the flowers are past their best. Petals curl up and begin to brown, leaves and stems are turned to gold and all manner of dark rust colours can be used.

Flower painting offers a good opportunity to paint in a free, spontaneous style. Rich mixes of colours can be used and allowed to run expressively on the paper. Accuracy is not of prime importance – at times it can even be a distraction. What is more important is to create a pleasing design and a picture that is lively and exuberant. I am particularly fond of painting marguerites and other daisy-type flowers because of their strong shape, especially when perfect blooms stand side by side with deadheads enjoying the last of the warm summer evenings.

Poppies Rose Madder was used to capture the rich colour of the poppy heads. The poppy leaves were a soft blue-green and were painted in lightly to contrast with the dark background (see page 80).

Poppies

30 × 45 centimetres (12 × 18 inches)

The painting (see page 79) has retained an unlaboured quality and freshness of colour, due mainly to careful masking-out before painting. To save time, I do not mask out whole flower heads, I just paint the masking fluid round the edge and take care when applying the washes not to go over the line.

The background is always exciting because I never know exactly how it is going to turn out. I try to inject as much spontaneity into the colours as possible. The great danger is in trying to do too much, then it starts to look laboured. Before the colours dried I scattered some salt into the blue at the top, creating a snowflake effect, simply to add to the textures. At this point it is probably a good idea to walk away for a while and let the colours settle because it is so tempting to intervene and help them on a bit.

When the paint was thoroughly dry the masking fluid was rubbed away. This painting was made on Saunders Rough paper so care had to be taken removing the masking fluid to avoid ripping the paper.

The leaves of the poppies were a soft blue-green and were painted in very lightly to contrast against the dark background. I made a point of leaving plenty of white patches amongst the leaves, where the sparkle of light broke through the foliage.

I chose Rose Madder for the poppy heads. This was painted in richly in some areas, with clear water added where the light caught the surface. A little Cadmium Yellow was used near the stems, gently blending into the red.

The colours used were Prussian Blue, Raw Sienna and Viridian for the background; French Ultramarine, Viridian and Opaque White for the foreground foliage; and Rose Madder, Cadmium Yellow and Prussian Blue for the flowers.

The Potted Plant

32 × 45 centimetres (13 × 18 inches)

This is as much a painting of a pot as of a plant (opposite). The simple heart-shaped leaves and the elegant contours of the pot are well defined against the dark background. Detail around the pot remains a little vague so that our attention is drawn to the leaves with their fine white veins.

Both pot and leaves were masked out to enable me to paint in the background unhindered. A rich mix of Intense

A rich, dark background offers a good contrast to the elegant contours of the pot and the simple heart-shaped leaves.

Blue, Indian Red and a little Raw Sienna made up the background colour. As I painted downward, I added more Indian Red and Raw Sienna to introduce the paved area behind. Before this dried I drew in the lines around the tiles with clear water, just enough to suggest their outline.

In the foreground, grass and weeds were masked out to enable me to paint this section broadly.

With the foreground and background complete, I could remove the masking fluid from the main subject. The pot was rubbed with candle wax and the surface brushed with clear water before the colours (Intense Blue, Viridian and Raw Sienna) were dropped in. At the lower corner, the terracotta colour was made from Naples Yellow and Cadmium Red Deep.

Each leaf of the plant was then painted separately, taking care to leave in the highlights and white veins.

At this point, I stood back to see where alterations needed to be made. I returned to painting the leaves, darkening sections here and there and adding a little more yellow to other areas. The colours used here were Viridian, Intense Blue, French Ultramarine and Cadmium Yellow.

Giant Hogweed

27 × 30 centimetres (11 × 12 inches)

Giant hogweed is a very impressive plant which towers above neighbouring plants. Unfortunately it is poisonous.

The plant was bathed in warm light as the sun sank behind the horizon. This is one of the best times to search for subjects to paint. The glow and the acute angle of the sun often provide atmospheric scenes.

The hogweed was painted in Raw Sienna and Burnt Sienna to capture the warm tones. The dark tones were painted in Burnt Umber with a touch of Viridian. The domes of the flower heads are made up of many smaller, coin-sized bunches. Their soft shape was achieved by running a wet brush around the outlines to make the paint run. Some highlights were created by lifting out paint with a brush, gently rubbing the spot with a brush of clear water then pressing a tissue against the area to lift the colours out.

This giant hogweed is bathed in the
glow of the setting sun. The softness of
the flower heads was achieved by
running a wet brush around the
outlines to make the paint run.

Broad strokes of the brush were used over a background wash and the wet-in-wet technique was employed on the terracotta pot.

Marguerites in an Old Pot

30 × 20 centimetres (12 × 8 inches)

Even a few straggly flowers like these can make an interesting little picture. The pale daisies are picked out against a dark background and an old flowerpot. This painting was made late in the afternoon with very dull light, hence the subdued colour. A larger painting of marguerites, with an explanation of the techniques used, can be seen on pages 87–89.

Black, grey and white pastel pencils are used to show contours, shading and highlighting in this sketch.

Detail of the painting opposite. Note how the white of the paper is used to highlight some of the petals. Subtle shading adds depth and shape to the flower.

Cardoon

17 × 20 centimetres (7 × 8 inches)

Cardoons produce massive seedheads surrounded by spiky outer petals, making an interesting subject to paint.

First I drew the seedhead, paying particular attention to the pattern of its structure. My initial brushstrokes were aimed at getting the basic shape and were applied briskly, taking care however not to overpaint the highlights on the upturned leaves.

With the basic shape painted in, I could start to describe each individual petal, the outlines of which could still be seen through the wash. When these were complete, I stepped back to see if I had made a convincing study. I made further adjustments, deepening the tones on the underside and adding more details where necessary. For this study I used just Raw Sienna, Burnt Sienna and French Ultramarine.

Marguerites

67 × 47 centimetres (27 × 19 inches)

Generally I find the larger a painting is, the greater the risks. This painting I would class as moderately large but I frequently work on paintings double this size. One of the risks is the formation of unsightly hard edges. This usually occurs at the edges of a wash but can also happen in unexpected areas due to uneven drying. The danger of this happening increases with larger paintings and can often ruin a good sky. By the time the problem is spotted, it is often too late to remedy it and an attempt at re-working just aggravates the situation.

To make this painting lively I have been very selective with the detail, masking out a few leaves and flowerheads. This has allowed me to use a large brush to paint in the background with rich mixes of Intense Blue, Viridian and Ivory Black. I applied the blue first then added the other colours, allowing them to run and mix on the paper. Brushloads of clear water were added to the top lefthand corner to create an area of highlight which drifted into the other colours, dislodging them slightly thus giving a strong feeling of movement and light. Further highlights were created by wiping out with a sponge.

The foreground is in fact very sparse. The flowerheads are mostly the white of the paper with splashes of colour coming from the yellow corollas. Despite the complete lack of detail, the mix of colours and the sprinkling of highlights gives the illusion of a busy flower border.

Opposite I used a limited palette for this study of a cardoon, with details added over a basic wash.

Marguerites The painting overleaf is very lively and a large brush was used to paint in the background. There is very little detail and the flower heads are suggested largely by the white of the paper.

Summer Flowers
Demonstration

27 × 44 centimetres (11 × 17¹/₂ inches)

Stage 1

The initial stage is straightforward. The flowers were drawn
and then painted out in masking fluid. I also flicked the brush
of masking fluid over the surface to give a speckle of highlights.

Selecting a 1 inch flat brush, I wet almost the entire
surface for the next step of wet-in-wet painting. This is exciting
and makes a welcome break from controlled techniques. I
loaded a size 14 brush with a mixture of Prussian Blue and a
little Cadmium Yellow, and applied it in broad sweeps across
the paper and round the flower heads. I allowed this to soak in
a little, then started to apply other colours – Raw Sienna and
Alizarin Crimson followed by some Viridian. Towards the top,
colours were flicked onto the paper from the brush. The
painting was then allowed to dry.

Stage 2

The masking fluid was rubbed away with a finger to leave the
white shapes of the flowers. The flower heads were painted in,
firstly with Cadmium Yellow. This was allowed to dry before
the second colour, Burnt Sienna and Burnt Umber, was painted
round each of them. The yellow centres were kept clear and all
the edges softened by applying a damp brush round them.

Stage 3

Each flower head was completed before I started painting in
the petals. For these, I combined Lemon Yellow with Cadmium
Orange to give some richer tones. The shaded sections were
painted in lightly with French Ultramarine.

Lastly the patina of seedheads was achieved by lifting out
tiny spots of paint. I do this with a fine wet brush, teasing spots
of paint until they lift, then immediately applying a tissue to
soak up the residue.

Opposite Stage 3 – the finished painting

Stage 1

Stage 2

TEN

Foregrounds and Undergrowth

This is often an area of dilemma for the watercolourist: with a loosely painted scene, should the foreground be painted in the same manner, or worked with more detail? Perhaps it should be left out altogether. Each painting will pose different problems. Often I am painting the foreground for its own sake, in which case the background might be left vague. Sometimes I find I like to paint a strong foreground while retaining a well defined distant view, as in my painting of Bourn (see page 97). At other times the foreground may be no more than a strong wash of colour.

It is possible to leave the foreground unresolved, particularly if there is nothing in that part of the painting that will enhance the scene. This can be done by adding washes and gently scrubbing the underlying colours with a brush so that colours lift and a fuzzy, out of focus effect develops. However it is treated the foreground is going to be a vital part of the painting and should be considered from the outset.

Overgrown Shed

24 × 15 centimetres (9¹/₂ × 6 inches)

This painting is quite small. Most of it was brushed in boldly wet-in-wet, mixing Viridian and Burnt Umber. This was followed by some delicate overpainting to define the foreground undergrowth.

An old shed hidden amongst foliage makes an interesting composition.

Hillside farm drawn in fine liner.

The detail in the undergrowth has been kept to a minimum and more attention has been paid to the rusty railings, where vibrant colours are used to enhance the shapes.

Iron Railings

45 × 27 centimetres (18 × 11 inches)

Fences are often contrived out of scrap material. These 'make do and mend' improvisations make good subjects for paintings and I am always on the look-out for examples. I have used the flat background of the river to give emphasis to the skeletal shapes of the fence and the confusion of undergrowth.

Rusty metal can have surprisingly bright colours. The colours I used in these railings were French Ultramarine, Cerulean Blue, Indian Red, Burnt Sienna, Raw Sienna and Naples Yellow. To ensure that the railings looked cylindrical I ran a brush along their length, picking up the excess paint and leaving a highlight. When dry, I used the dry-brush technique to rub in patches of rust, taking care to keep the colours bright.

The undergrowth has been painted more broadly, the detail added by overpainting in gouache. Detail is vague here to avoid attention being drawn away from the railings.

The Church at Bourn

62 × 32 centimetres (25 × 13 inches)

To get this interesting view of the church (overleaf) it was necessary to get down low so that I was looking through the undergrowth at the edge of a field, with the church and vicarage held in a band of light across the centre of the scene. A break in the clouds draws our attention to the steeple, which has a most unusual twist – it is not an error of draughtsmanship!

Foreground detail is important when searching for elements to bring a landscape to life. Simple things like a branch in the foreground can help lead the eye into the picture.

The foreground in this scene is very dark, so I mixed a wash of Burnt Umber and a little Ivory Black for the deep tones. As I laid the colour down, I softened the top edge of the wash with a brush of clear water so that I did not have an ugly hard edge where the light and dark sections meet. When this was dry I developed the dark area by painting in leaves, twigs and stems silhouetted against the background. Lighter areas were brought in by overpainting in gouache opaque colours – some dark green bramble leaves dabbed in on the left and faint areas of green grass drawn in. Lastly I painted in the tall grasses catching the last of the sun. Here I used a rigger paintbrush, which is ideal for long, thin lines.

In these details (above and below right) the fine grass stalks are in opaque paint, contrasting light against dark. Where the warm rays of the sun caught the stems they were painted in Naples Yellow with a little red added. In the lower, shaded area, cool colours were mixed from Opaque White, French Ultramarine and Raw Sienna.

The Church at Bourn The evening
sun casts a glow over the landscape. A
fair amount of detail is shown, with the
foreground hedges receding into the
distance. Colours in the distance are
softened by adding Chinese White to
the paint.

View Across Fields, Tralee

30 × 45 centimetres (12 × 18 inches)

I often use lanes and streams as a way of leading the eye into a painting but few are as spectacular as this track running down a hillside near Tralee in Southern Ireland. At the end of the lane is a road which is reflecting the sun, giving one bright spot of highlight in the centre of the picture. The rest of the scene is bathed in a warm glow of light from the evening sun, its rays filtering through the edge and casting shadows across the lane.

The lane points to the chequerboard of fields in the distance, broken up here and there by the occasional tree. The foreground hedges are painted distinctly but as they recede into the distance their definition becomes faint. I find a useful way of softening colours in the distance is to add some Chinese White to the paint rather than just diluting it with water. This gives the colours a little body and makes these passages somewhat more positive in effect.

Opposite Lanes and pathways are a useful compositional feature. They lead the eye gently into the painting, as in this straight path here.

The mill at Sutton Mandeville, painted in black watercolour.

Winding Track

22 × 27 centimetres (9 × 11 inches)

Grass can be difficult to portray convincingly. I use various techniques, some of which are illustrated in this picture.

The entire foreground was painted with a mixture of Raw Sienna and Burnt Sienna. Candle wax was rubbed along the track first, causing the paint to speckle. On top of this warm rust-coloured wash I brushed over some Burnt Sienna and Viridian. When dry, the tones were lowered by brushing French Ultramarine into the areas of grass and allowing it to dry. Over this brushstrokes of brilliant green mixed with Chinese White were applied. The amount of green has to be carefully measured as it can easily veer to chocolate-box hues. Lastly fine adjustments were made – adding a little white body colour here and there, softening edges by rubbing them with a wet brush, and drawing in some blades of grass with a fine brush charged with a mix of Chinese White, Viridian and Brilliant Green.

Opposite A winding path leads the eye to the view beyond the gate, where detail is kept to a minimum. Foliage and grass colours are built up in the foreground with fine detail added on top.

In this pen and ink sketch the foreground detail is applied loosely to create areas of light and dark.

The details here were created by overpainting. Foliage
overlays leaves which fall over the mud bank. The
reeds are built up with long strokes of the brush.

Reflected Fence

30 × 22 centimetres (12 × 9 inches)

Though the water is casting a mirror-like reflection and the scene is very still, there is nevertheless a lot of movement within this composition. At the top of the picture the reeds lean over to the left, followed by their reflection. The railings lean to the right and likewise are followed by a reverse image in the water. The result is rather like a herringbone design, full of diagonal lines. Diagonal lines within a composition denote dynamism and activity, while irregular horizontal lines tend to convey tranquillity.

Most of the detail within the painting has been achieved through overpainting, mixing Opaque White or Naples Yellow with touches of the appropriate colour. The background reeds are Opaque White mixed with Viridian and French Ultramarine, the foreground leaves are Opaque White with Leaf Green, and the straw colour of old grass stems is made from Naples Yellow.

The old bridge at Harrold, drawn with a technical pen.

Stage 1

Stage 2

Stage 3

Stage 4 – the finished painting,
see page 106.

Country Path
Demonstration

29 × 42 centimetres (11¹/₂ × 17 inches)

Stage 1

After drawing the scene and masking out some details, I applied a broad wash of French Ultramarine. While wet, the background hills and banks to the left were painted in French Ultramarine and Raw Sienna, allowing the colours to blend in softly with the sky. While this was drying, I painted in the bank on the right with a rich mix of Sap Green, Burnt Sienna and French Ultramarine.

Stage 2

I rubbed candle wax over the trunk of the tree to break up the paint and give the quality of bark. Raw Sienna, Burnt Sienna and Sap Green were then applied to the lefthand side of the trunk and brushed with clear water to encourage the colours to spread to the other side of the trunk and give a feeling of solidity to the tree.

Stage 3

The branches and twigs could then be painted, varying the colours between French Ultramarine, Raw Sienna and Burnt Sienna. Some of the large branches were painted in the same manner as the trunk to impart a roundness to them.

Stage 4

In this final stage (see overleaf) the branches are completed. The masking fluid in the foreground was removed and detail added to the scene. Some of the detailing has been painted in with gouache, mixing small quantities of water to Naples Yellow gouache to get the correct pigment for the strands of dead grass. The path was painted in with French Ultramarine and Raw Sienna, leaving strips of white paper at the far end of the lane to give an impression of bands of light.

Finally the textures in the lane and the dapple of green undergrowth in the foreground were all judiciously added by overpainting in gouache.

ELEVEN

Reflections

Watercolour is the perfect medium for conveying the qualities of water and reflections. The subtle effects of light playing on water and the meaning of colours are ideally suited to the skills of wet-in-wet painting.

Once your interest in water has been awakened you will begin to see its potential in less obvious images, such as rain-filled puddles or rutted paths. Even street scenes are transformed in a shower of rain, with the shop windows and lights creating a dazzle of colour.

Village Church
Reflections in a river are shown here using the wet-in-wet technique.

Boats on the Cam

62 × 45 centimetres (25 × 18 inches)

I tend to divide paintings up into sections as I work. This way I can retain control and do not end up with so many things going on in the painting that I cannot give my full attention to critical areas. Here I would divide the background into blocks – the dark area to the left, followed by the brickwork, and then the bush and grass to the right. The next section would be the rowing boats.

The area that cannot be divided up and will create problems is the water. This has to be completed in one go and has to be worked quickly to avoid hard edges forming.

First masking fluid was applied to mask out a scattering of white dots and the reeds draped along the surface of the water. This was followed by a wash of French Ultramarine, which I immediately began to work over to create the dark reflections of the boats and the background foliage. The stern of the boat in the foreground was painted in Naples Yellow, worked in wet-in-wet to give it a soft outline. I used a Japanese bamboo brush to give a ragged edge to the reflection. Some areas are soft-edged, while to the left the wash of French Ultramarine had already dried and so the reflection is more hard-edged. Finally I allowed the colours to dry before removing the masking fluid and touching in the reeds.

Lake Lyndon

65 × 45 centimetres (26 × 18 inches)

The painting on pages 110 and 111 is a good example of 'scrubbing-out'. Practise this technique on a discarded painting because it can easily go wrong and ruin a good painting.

Sometimes a large area of water can look a bit leaden so to add some atmosphere I introduced a shaft of light across the water. There are a number of ways this can be done. It can be painted out in masking fluid at the very start of the painting; this will leave a very sharp-edged band of light. Another way is to scrape it out with a razor blade; this can work well, leaving a speckle of highlights, but it will damage the surface of the paper. I chose to scrub it out as this would leave a soft-edged band of light, more suitable for this moody evening scene.

I selected a small bristle brush, wet it and dragged it across the paper two or three times. I then dried the brush on a tissue, re-wet it and did the same again. Most of the paint should have lifted off by then and could be soaked up by the brush.

I created the dark reflections in this painting using a basic wash of French Ultramarine and applying colour on top.

Overleaf To add atmosphere to the
painting I scrubbed out an area of highlight
across the water using a small wet
bristle brush. Keeping the line straight
is difficult, but the effect works well.

Water-filled Tracks

15 × 22 centimetres (6 × 9 inches)

This is a good example of loose, bold brushwork followed by fine detail work. The painting is divided into three sections – sky, landscape and the pools of water in the tractor tracks. Working systematically, it can be achieved without having a laboured quality.

The pools of water were masked out so that I could forget about them while on the landscape section. This was put in very quickly, starting with the distant hedgerow. The top of the hedgerow was softened by brushing some clear water across the top edge of the wet paint.

The areas of reddish earth were painted in with a mix of Burnt Sienna, Indian Red and French Ultramarine. While this was still wet Raw Sienna was brushed into the remaining areas, blending into the red earth colours. Before drying was complete the greens were added, using Winsor Green and Burnt Sienna – Winsor Green can be rather strident so it needs to be used sparingly.

Now that all the base work was completed I was able to work on the detail, starting with the hedgerow in the background. The hair-like brushstrokes making up the trees and branches were put in with a size 2 long-haired sable brush. As I worked down through the picture I began to describe the irregularities on the verges, the patches of soil showing through the grass and the ruts in the path.

With much of the work completed I could now remove the masking fluid and paint in the water-filled ruts. I mixed French Ultramarine with a touch of Burnt Sienna to give a silver-grey. The colours were applied more strongly in the foreground as this helped to lead into the picture, then further stripes of colour were applied to convey the quality of water.

I used gouache opaque paints to introduce some of the fine details. The straw-coloured grass stems were painted in with Naples Yellow. The same colour mixed with a little red was used to create the highlight on the path where some rays of light cut across the tracks, and also where the tractor had formed ridges in the mud.

The water-filled ruts are a prominent feature of this painting. Fine detail is added to the grassy banks and the distant hedgerows and trees.

Shady Pool

29 × 21 centimetres (11 1/2 × 8 1/2 inches)

The play of light as it filters through trees and sparkles on wet stones is a theme that always attracts painters. Detail has been kept to a minimum so that the softness of the scene is not lost. Here and there I have picked out a few twigs and a scattering of leaves where the light catches them. The foliage was painted very loosely but defined afterwards with a little overpainting, mixing Viridian with Opaque White for the light greens and Indian Red with Viridian for the dark greens.

River Bank

20 × 29 centimetres (8 × 11 1/2 inches)

The tranquil of the river bank setting on page 116 has no particular defined features to catch our attention, just the overall atmosphere of cool greens and grey skies reflecting into the slow waters of the Ouse.

 The overall painting was washed in, with the foliage of the trees dabbed on in the split-brush technique. Branches and boughs were then introduced, the main tree in the foreground being painted in Burnt Sienna and French Ultramarine. Using a size 6 brush, I started to pick out some of the leaves in Viridian and Burnt Umber. Lighter leaves were touched in with Opaque White and Viridian. Finally the reeds were painted in with a mix of Opaque White and Leaf Green, taking care to mirror their reflections in the water.

Light and shade intermingle in this painting of a shady pool protected by rocky banks and a canopy of leaves. Details are painted over washes of colour.

River Bank Cool greens and grey
skies are reflected in the slow-moving
river. The split-brush technique is used
for the foliage and the reeds are
painted in using a rigger.

TWELVE

Coastal Scenes

The coast and inland waterways provide an endlessly changing source of material for paintings. Beached hulls, mud, pools of water, the sparkle of light playing gently on the waves, and mirror images reflected in the water — these are all subjects that seem to cry out to be painted in watercolour. Certainly the combination of water, the elements and boats has been enough to keep many artists absorbed for a lifetime.

I am particularly fond of these scenes because there is always an air of decay and disorder. However hard people try, the sea ensures a lack of uniformity and a constant chaos of ropes and debris amongst the mudpools. Boats add a splash of colour to any painting, and the sea, beaches and mud flats offer many subjects for the painter. I have chosen several subjects for this section, including pools of water and boats left behind in sunlit mudflats, and a patch of sand littered with shells.

Fishing Boat

31 × 26 centimetres (12¹/₂ × 10¹/₂ inches)

This fishing boat made a splash of colour as it sat in the mud of an estuary.

The red flank of the hull was painted in Vermilion, followed by the addition of Cadmium Red and French Ultramarine for the darker tones. The colours were worked in wet-in-wet so that they would run together, emphasizing the roundness of the hull. I find care has to be taken with reds — it only takes a small contamination from other colours to turn reds to browns. When using bright colours, it pays to err on the side of brightness as colours can easily be toned down later.

I rubbed candle wax over the foreground before painting to give a gritty texture to the paint, which would help describe the surface of the mud. The colours used for this section were Burnt Sienna, Cadmium Red and French Ultramarine.

Boats drawn in marker pen on pastel paper.

A fishing boat adds a splash of colour. Candle wax was rubbed over the foreground area before painting, to add texture to the mud.

Study of reflections,
drawn with a
technical pen.

Mudflats

45 × 57 centimetres (18 × 23 inches)

In this painting I was attracted to the pools of water that the tide left behind, each pool glistening with the reflection of the sky.

Care was taken at the drawing stage as close attention was needed to draw the subtle curves of the boat hulls accurately. I drew the outlines of the puddles as I wanted the reflections to be accurate. The next stage was to paint masking fluid over all the detailed sections so that I could paint the mudflats freely without having to run the brush round the awkward edges of the two boats and the numerous puddles. To paint the mudflats, I chose a 1 inch flat brush so that I could apply the paint quickly. Starting from the top, I ran a wash of Naples Yellow and Raw Sienna across the paper, sweeping the brush from right to left and tilting the board towards me slightly to encourage the paint to run down. Before the wash dried, I applied more colours, deepening those in the foreground and creating bands of shadow near the water's edge. These deeper tones were a mix of Burnt Sienna and French Ultramarine. The washes were allowed to dry before more detailed work was done to paint in the ridges and dimples.

I could now remove some of the masking fluid so that I could work on the boats, but I left the masking fluid in place on the mudflats in case I wanted to make changes later.

The boat in the foreground was mainly painted in Cerulean Blue mixed with a little Raw Sienna, the shadows added by mixing Cerulean Blue with some Burnt Sienna and French Ultramarine. Detailing the boat involved adding all the little blemishes, such as the peeling paint and rust stains on the hull. A little Sap Green was used where the underside of the boat had been submerged.

The green boat was a mix of Burnt Umber and Viridian, painted on in quite a thick mix, allowed to dry, then lightened in some areas by lifting paint out with a brush. The tyre on the side of the boat was treated in a similar manner, lifting out the highlights.

The shadows beneath the boats were the kind of danger area where a simple mistake can ruin a painting. The

The white of the paper is used to capture the feeling of water trapped in the mud flats. The puddles were masked out before painting to retain their interesting shapes.

Detail of the painting on the previous page.

foreground shadow was the hardest because it faded out as it extended towards me. I mixed French Ultramarine with Burnt Sienna and painted the shadow, feathering it as it faded out towards me and adding clear water to soften the edge. When dry, a darker rim of colour was applied to the edge of the shadow where it met the boat, helping to emphasize the roundness of the hull. Then with care I used a brush to lift out a highlight that was reflected down from the flank of the boat into the wet sand.

When all the painting was completed, I could at last remove the masking fluid that covered the pools of water, revealing white patches of paper.

Study of weathered wood, drawn with a technical pen.

Beachcombing

30 × 22 centimetres (12 × 9 inches)

There were a number of ways I could have painted this patch of beach to give an impression of sand. One would have been to stipple with a fine brush but this would have taken a long time. Another would have been to use the split-brush technique which I use for foliage but the tiny points of paint from this technique tend to be elongated and not suitable in this scene. I chose instead to spatter the paint on to create the desired effect.

As there is little control over where the dots will land, I masked out everything other than the sand in masking fluid. I then covered the paper in a wash of Naples Yellow followed by an additional wash of Indian Red and French Ultramarine in a very weak mix to give me the base colours.

The spattering was achieved by tapping the brush with a finger in the same manner a smoker does to dislodge ash from a cigarette. Too wet a brush will result in large droplets of paint landing on the painting, so it is a good idea to experiment on a sheet of waste paper first.

When the base paint was dry I mixed some Raw Sienna in the palette with a size 6 brush, removed excess paint on the side of the palette and began to spatter. I held the brush a few inches from the surface of the paper and spread the dots randomly across the surface. After the Raw Sienna I followed with other colours – French Ultramarine, Cerulean Blue, Burnt Sienna, Ivory Black and Sap Green – until there was a rich blend of colours on the paper.

The last stage was to remove the masking fluid and paint in the scattered shells and the dead crab. I paid particular attention to the shadows, underpinning the three-dimensional shapes and giving them sharp definition against the flatness of the background.

Paint was spattered onto the paper over two washes of colour, to create a sandy, textured feel.

124

This detail shows
how the surface
quality of the sand
has been built up
with layers of
different coloured
dots.

A painting of a young boy with a traction engine. Detail is added as the layers of paint are built up.

The Traction Engine

29 × 20 centimetres (11¹/₂ × 8 inches)

I wanted this painting to be a true likeness so I concentrated most of my efforts on the features, gently adding colour in thin washes to build up the skin colours.

Building up colours in layers of wash can be difficult because of the possibility of lifting colours underneath. To avoid this, I work to a strict rule and that is only to allow the brush to pass over a section of the painting once. If a second brushstroke is made, it will very likely lift the colours from underneath. After each glaze, I allow the painting to dry before adding the next.

Index